JOIN THE REDEFINING NORMAL MOVEMENT

READY TO REDEFINE NORMAL?

FAITH-BASED EDITION

I0082115

COMPANION GUIDE TO REDEFINING NORMAL
BY JUSTIN & ALEXIS BLACK

CONTENTS

DISCLAIMER

This companion guide performs best in combination with receiving services from a therapist, counselor, or trusted adult. The work includes many topics that may need support and clarification from professional mental health resources.

INTRODUCTION

The journey of self-discovery that Alexis and Justin experienced may be similar to the one you find yourself traveling. This companion guide is an extension of the Redefining Normal book. Through this book, you will be challenged to explore your faith journey in order to utilize those lessons and strategies in real world settings. This book is not meant to replace counseling or other means of support, but rather to be used as a tool while working with supportive people and organizations.

This book will provide you guidance on how to serve communities and individuals starting with personal self-reflection and the connectivity of service and God's purpose for our lives.

Some of the questions are very personal, so make sure you are in a safe place both mentally and physically before beginning this journey. Also, feel free to skip any question you are not prepared for and return to it later.

Invite the Holy Spirit to be your Counselor (John 14:26 - "But the Advocate, the Holy Spirit, whom the Father will send in my name, will teach you all things and will remind you of everything I have said to you," NIV). While we invite the Holy Spirit into our journey, we are ultimately in control of which direction we take in the journey. If you know you are in a vulnerable and wounded place, we encourage you to seek Godly counsel about when, where and how much you read on your own.

These questions and activities are intended to help you examine your areas of growth and how we can channel our spiritual gifts and resources into creating communities that reflect the Kingdom of God and building individuals that operate outside the lens of trauma.

Reading and answering these questions are intended to make you aware of how to influence youth and individuals who have experienced generational trauma.

God has great plans for you (Jeremiah 29:11) and those who come after you!

("For I will pour water on the thirsty land, and streams on the dry ground; I will pour out my Spirit on your offspring, and my blessing on your descendants," Isaiah 44:3, NIV)

This guide will give you perspective on:

1. Creating generational success for families, youth, and adults who've experienced trauma starting with personal development.
2. Helping the foster care system in Foster/Adopted/Kinship (FAK) family situations with caretakers other than their biological parents.
3. Understanding God's purpose for families and communities in despair.

"We hope that by sharing what we have experienced, we can save others from going through similar heartache." ~Alexis and Justin Black

HOW TO USE THIS GUIDE

It can be used in various ways including as a guide for individuals, couples, married couples, etc. If you need more guidance, here is how you can use it for a group:

The Group Experience
The Session Format
The Group Leader

Trigger Warning

Go at your own pace through the workbook. We encourage each individual to decide on a comfortable pace in which you can understand and process the questions and information that we discuss. We encourage you to also identify a person whom you trust to talk about potential triggers or emotional distress if they happen. Let your person know you are working through this book and that you might rely on them as a resource when you feel unsettled. In addition, use your other health strategies to settle yourself.

This book has a "trigger warning" for its content of discussing a variety of situations related to sexual and abusive situations.

A trigger warning is an alert to the reader or viewer to the fact that it contains potentially distressing material.

What do you expect to feel when reading these parts of the book? Does just seeing the words "trigger warning" make you feel uncomfortable?

_____

_____

_____

_____

Is the Holy Spirit giving you a:
- Green light (continue)
- Yellow light (proceed with caution/with counsel)
- Red light (stop; don't continue reading today)

READING SCHEDULE

If you haven't already read it

SESSION 1 Words on an Index Card

SESSION 2 Identity
"What Did They Tell Me About My Identity?" | "Desperate for Love" | "Worthiness"

SESSION 3 Redefining Normal: Definition of Love
"Sell-out" | "The Cycle" | "Turning Point"

SESSION 4 Redefining Normal: Breaking Cycles Part 1
"Revealing the Truth in My Trauma" | "Vulnerable Through the Pain" | "Mental Warfare"| "True Colors" | "Self-Sabotage" | "Imago"

SESSION 5 Redefining Normal: Breaking Cycles Part 2
"Sacrifice & Submission" | "Talk it Out" | "City Kids Travel the Globe" | "The Proposal" | "Love is Not Always Black & White"

SESSION 6 Redefining Normal: Agreement
"Intentionality" | "Foundation" | "Oneness" | "I'm Not Your Enemy" | "Friends First" | "Building a Legacy" | "The Two Shall be One" | "What's Next" | "Epilogue"

WHAT IS REDEFINING NORMAL?

Your "normal" has been shaped by your family, community, and society. The meaning of normal is to conform to a standard; usual, typical, or expected. As former foster youth, Justin and Alexis inherited a culture of ideas that was a reflection of the trauma within their family and community. This generational "normal" became their reality and the image they had of themselves. This became their normal and generational trauma they had grown accustomed to.

Seeing life through YOUR "normal" is like looking through a lens in a pair of glasses. What is your perception? How are experiences framed for you? Do you experience relationships through a healed heart or a wounded heart? Do you view yourself, challenges and victories through your past, people and experiences you've had, or through God's Word and His truth about you?

Though you may or may not have experienced trauma or the child welfare system, this workbook encourages readers to be self-reflective and analyze the aspects that determine your character and who you are fundamentally. Chances are, you or someone you know may have experienced traumatic beginnings or time in the foster care system. We also encourage individuals to be aware of the cultural foundation of their family and examine the complexities that shape their relationships.

This workbook will help you build and strengthen a sense of control, autonomy, and excitement to establish a more conductive pathway for yourself and the generations after you.

DEFINING TRAUMA

"Experiences are considered traumatic when they threaten the life or physical integrity of the child or of someone critically important to the child (such as a parents, grandparent or sibling)."

ACTIVITY

Given the concept of "normal", how would you describe your normal? These may consist of the expectation set before you by family, your community, and society. Things to consider when describing your normal is your age, race, gender, income status, etc.

_____

_____

_____

_____

_____

_____

_____

_____

_____

_____

_____

_____

When you think about the definition of trauma, do you know any one who's familiar with those experiences?

_____

_____

_____

_____

_____

_____

What does redefining your "normal" mean to you?

_____

_____

_____

_____

_____

_____

Words on an Index Card

_____

Based on the Redefining Normal "Words on an Index Card"

SESSION AIM:

Opening up about past experiences and starting to share stories.

WHAT THE STATISTICS SAY:

65% of children in foster care experience seven or more school changes from elementary to high school. Foster youth lose between four and six months of educational progress with each school change.

Only 56% of foster youth graduate high school; less than 3% of foster youth graduate from college.

ADVERSE CHILDHOOD EXPERIENCES (ACES).

Have you ever heard of ACE's? These have a tremendous impact on future violence, victimization and perpetration, and lifelong health and opportunity. An ACE score (0 to 10) is a tally of different types of abuse, neglect, and other hallmarks of a rough childhood. According to the Adverse Childhood Experiences Study, the rougher your childhood, the higher your score is likely to be and the higher your risk for later health problems such as alcoholism, obesity, drug use, depression, suicide attempts, cancer, heart disease, and more.

Approximately 2/3 of participants had at least one ACE; 1 in 5 had 3 or more ACE's. Widespread prevalence of childhood exposure to trauma—cuts across race and class lines. As ACE's increase, so do the risk factors for a variety of health and wellbeing problems (CDC, 2019).

"For those of us who have been traumatized in our youth, we have to redefine ourselves and redefine what is normal." - Justin

Justin has a score of 9 and Alexis a 10…

To know your ACEs score, search 'NPR ACEs Quiz' and take the test.

STARTER QUESTION

Relationships are all different. We believe parents display the first example of a relationship, while the relationship between children and parents dictates the future romantic relationships for their child. Our definitions of love are created and displayed by our parental figures. But has that definition been conducive and productive for us personally, professionally, and spiritually?

"We had to go through individual journeys to define who we are, our values, and our own healing before coming together. We couldn't do any of those things for each other. Just as we couldn't rely on our partner to make us happy. We had to find ways to make ourselves happy."
- Alexis

STEP 1
PERSONAL NEED

Reflect on the initial moment that inspired you to do the work that you do. That defining moment, and it may have been a couple or a series of events. It may be difficult to think about the exact moment but think about it for a second. The first story that you heard, that initial conversation that sparked your interest. Maybe even a statistic that you saw. . .

That moment made me feel _____

Which inspired me to then _____

While hoping to inspire others to _____

Ultimately, it is necessary for each individual to identify their own definition of individual happiness. If external sources become the foundation of our happiness, then we fall victim to being controlled by our circumstances and individuals around us. What components of your definition are you at odds with? Who/what do you believe/feel is in control of your happiness? How does that impact your decision-making or general satisfaction with life?

"'Well done, good and faithful servant! You have been faithful with a few things; I will put you in charge of many things. Come and share your master's happiness!'"
Matthew 25:23NIV

Example:

I am on the journey to find *(happiness/success/contentment)*. *(Getting my education/finding supportive friends/isolating myself)* is what I've done to pursue it, because I have struggled with *(understanding my purpose/feeling secure/opening up to others)*. *(Hope/confidence/self-love)* is the foundational piece that I am missing and *(fear/resentment/doubt)* is holding me back from reaching it.

You are welcome to fill in the blanks with your own words or from the example.

I am on the journey to find _____. _____ is what I've done to pursue it, because I have struggled with _____. _____ is the foundational piece that I am missing and _____ is holding me back from reaching it.

PROCESS OF HEALING

Identify the things, people, and resources that have contributed to your mental or emotional growth.

1. _____

2. _____

3. _____

4. _____

Who/what formed your perspective of mental health and how do you believe mental health ties to spiritual growth?

Note: We invite you to be vulnerable in your experiences. What has the world told you should be fulfilling and make you happy? Personalize your answers:

_____

_____

_____

_____

_____

_____

_____

_____

_____

_____

Many times we are pursuing pre-existing goals and expectations that were set before us; a pathway that wasn't made or fitting for us. This means that meeting the expectations of someone else frequently only results in outward satisfaction and not internal validation. This can affect your long-term personal satisfaction.

Contentment is tied to understanding purpose, identity, and personal satisfaction

1. The ability to change our perspective of our barriers shapes identity.
   "Consider it pure joy, my brothers and sisters, whenever you face trials of many kinds, because you know that the testing of your faith produces perseverance. Let perseverance finish its work so that you may be mature and complete, not lacking anything." (James 1:2-4 NIV)

2. Discovering a problem gives you an advantage of solving which helps you understand your purpose.
   "Not only so, but we also glory in our sufferings, because we know that suffering produces perseverance; perseverance, character; and character, hope," (Romans 5:3-4, NIV)

3. Have confidence in the end result. Be confident in God's ability to help you achieve success and find contentment in your pursuit.
   "Trust in the Lord with all your heart and lean not on your own understanding;in all your ways submit to him,and he will make your paths straight," (Proverbs 3:5, 6, NIV)

STEP 2
GROUP DISCUSSION

When you hear about the role that Alexis's foster parents had in their story, what do you notice? When they offered help, what boundaries and communication style did they use? In what ways did it differ from her upbringing with her biological parents?

(discuss with a group)

_____

_____

_____

_____

List three things that are keeping you from contentment.

1. _____

2. _____

3. _____

"But godliness with contentment is great gain. For we brought nothing into the world, and we can take nothing out of it. But if we have food and clothing, we will be content with that. Those who want to get rich fall into temptation and a trap and into many foolish and harmful desires that plunge people into ruin and destruction. For the love of money is a root of all kinds of evil. Some people, eager for money, have wandered from the faith and pierced themselves with many griefs. But you, man of God, flee from all this, and pursue righteousness, godliness, faith, love, endurance and gentleness." (1 Timothy 6:6-11 NIV.)

ACTIVITY

On your own, take a moment to fill in the white index card outline below. If you are doing this in a group setting, be sure to crease and tear off to hand to your discussion group leader to read anonymously later on:

WRITE DOWN something you've been through that people wouldn't know by looking at you.
(E.g., family trauma, sexual trauma, mental illness, trouble with friends, school trouble, etc.)

_____

_____

_____

_____

_____

_____

_____

_____

_____

_____

_____

_____

_____

The purpose of this activity is NOT to remind you of previous trauma, but instead encourage you along your journey, reminding you how far you've come!

In the bag below, write or draw a few of the things that you have been told, or feel, is your "baggage".

As a group, this activity helps individuals get to know one another while showcasing the commonalities they share. It can also encourage individuals to share facts about themselves that they might not consider revealing unprompted.

_____

_____

_____

_____

_____

_____

_____

_____

_____

_____

_____

_____

_____

_____

_____

_____

_____

_____

_____

_____

What parts of your journey do you try to hide when meeting new people?

_____

_____

_____

_____

_____

_____

_____

_____

What fears do you have about sharing parts of your journey?

_____

_____

_____

_____

_____

_____

_____

_____

_____

List the pros and cons from sharing your journey.

Pros

_____

_____

_____

_____

_____

_____

_____

_____

_____

Cons

_____

_____

_____

_____

_____

_____

_____

_____

_____

Do you believe that hiding pieces of your journey indirectly impacts new relationships? Why or Why not?

_____

_____

_____

_____

Sometimes we overshare or undershare in relationships. In what ways do you know when there are safe people to share with?

_____

_____

_____

_____

How do you believe your testimony could impact new believers and people who are struggling with their faith?

_____

_____

_____

_____

"Therefore, if anyone is in Christ, he is a new creation. The old has passed away; behold, the new has come."
2 Corinthians 5:17

Use the outline of a person below and draw the things, people, and opportunities that have helped you become the person you are today, or the things you need for continuous growth (Example: graduation cap, family members, bible study groups, counseling etc.).

Take time to really be specific. Of course we are all in need of the word of God and His spirit, but what activities and practices continue to help you along your journey?

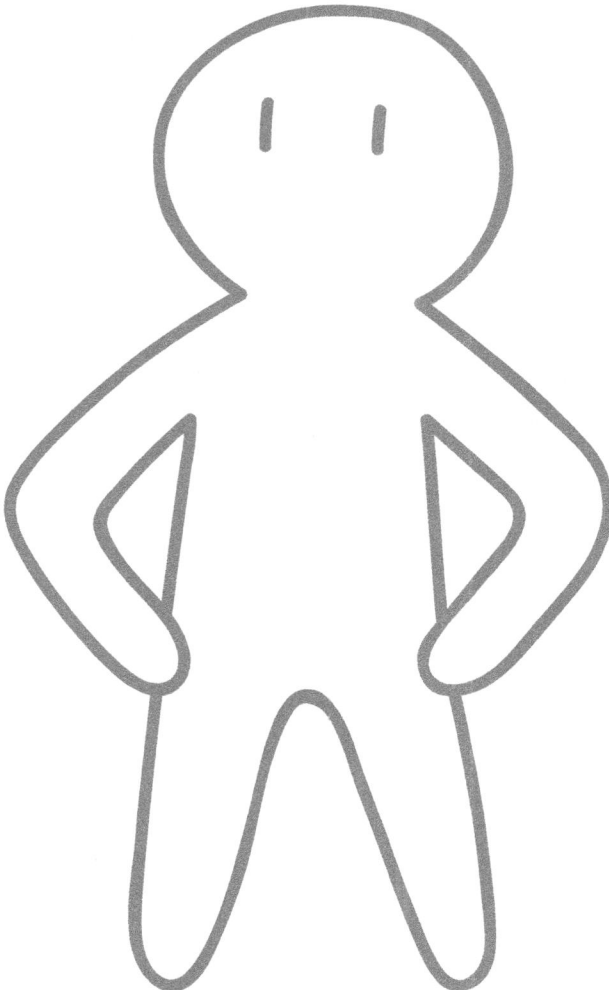

What was your reasoning for making a change in life? What was hard and what did you learn about yourself during that time?

_____

_____

_____

_____

_____

_____

_____

_____

Carrying your relationship with the Lord into new situations where people don't know you can be challenging. What do you want others to know about you and your faith? What have you kept hidden and why?

_____

_____

_____

_____

_____

_____

_____

Have you ever found yourself wanting to fit in, be wanted, or to feel important to someone else, so much that you were willing to hurt yourself or deny God's calling? Take a few moments to break it down in steps:

1. What have you craved from others in the past? Example: *Love, affection, attention, acknowledgement.* This could include family, friends, and romantic partners. Identify what was the craving and who was it from.

_____

_____

_____

2. What did you sacrifice or alter about your integrity to get it?

_____

_____

_____

3. What was the outcome?

_____

_____

_____

4. Knowing what you know now, how would you approach it differently next time?

_____

_____

_____

SETTING YOUR EXPECTATIONS

1. Some people have unrealistic expectations for us while others expect us to fall in line to the ways in which the world operates. As believers, it's important that we ask the Lord what He desires for us to do in life.

   "Whatever you do, work at it with all your heart, as working for the LORD, not for human masters, since you know that you will receive an inheritance from the LORD as a reward. It is the LORD Christ you are serving." ~ Colossians 3:23

   "Be devoted to one another in love. Honor one another above yourselves" - Romans 12:10

2. Setting our mind on Christ and identifying what is satisfactory to the spirit of God, setting daily goals will bring about happiness. Make a steady process and enjoy what you've accomplished today. Ask the Lord what His goals for you today are. We may set out on a day thinking the day will be to check specific items off on our to do list... but the Lord may have other plans. It's important that we connect with Him while still intending to accomplish the daily goals we set for ourselves.

   "But the fruit of the Spirit is love, joy, peace, forbearance, kindness, goodness, faithfulness, gentleness and self-control. Against such things there is no law." (Galatians 5:22-23NIV)

3. Learn to set expectations for yourself that challenge you and overcome fear.

Reflect on what has gotten you to this point and what will INSTEAD carry you forward on your pursuit of expanding the kingdom of God while displaying his grace and mercy!

SETTING EXPECTATIONS PT. 2

1. Every day, do something that brings about fulfillment: Scripture to start your day, exercising, eating healthy, starting a gratitude journal, having a sleep schedule. These are some intentional practices that can contribute to the well-being of your mind, body, and spirit.

2. Make sure these activities are not harmful to your mental, physical, or emotional well-being. Though we encourage activities that are self-satisfying, be aware that activities that inflict self-harm may feel good temporarily but could cause long-term or permanent damage. Refer to your primary care physician for additional activity that can healthily contribute to your mental, physical, and emotional well-being.

3. Learn to enjoy the process of mental and spiritual growth. Don't get too consumed with end results. Truth be told, the journey will be a lot longer than the conclusion, so enjoy the journey instead! This may require a mindset shift as we approach the process of serving God's purpose instead of our own..

"If you keep my commands, you will remain in my love, just as I have kept my Father's commands and remain in his love. I have told you this so that my joy may be in you and that your joy may be complete." (John 15:10-11NIV)

Small steps are okay!! If you are afraid, ask the Lord for a revelation of His perfect love for you!

"And so we know and rely on the love God has for us.
God is love. Whoever lives in love lives in God, and God in them. This is how love is made complete among us so that we will have confidence on the day of judgment: In this world we are like Jesus. There is no fear in love. But perfect love drives out fear, because fear has to do with punishment. The one who fears is not made perfect in love." 1 John 4:16-18

When you think of intimacy and vulnerability, what boundaries do you think are paired with them? How are those communicated, and when, for healthy relationships to form?

_____

_____

_____

_____

_____

Have there been experiences in your past that would be too painful to have read out loud even with anonymity? What perceived barriers do you have to healing from these experiences?

_____

_____

_____

_____

_____

TAKE A BREAK

We understand that discussing these topics as it relates to your experiences can be difficult. Please take a moment to decompress by taking 5 deep breaths.

CALM DOWN WITH TAKE 5 BREATHING

How do you feel now? Are you calm or would you like to take another 5 breaths?

1. Stretch your hand out like a star.
2. Get the pointer finger of your other hand ready to trace your fingers up and down.
3. Slide up each finger slowly ~ slide down the other side.
4. Breathe in through your nose ~ out through your mouth.
5. Put it together and breathe in as you slide up and breathe out as you slide down.
   Keep going until you have finished tracing your hand.

© childhood101.com

SESSION 2
REDEFINING NORMAL

Identity

Based on Redefining Normal Identity:
"What Did They Tell Me About My Identity?" | "Desperate for
Love" | "Worthiness"

SESSION AIM:

Understanding our desire for love, and learn more about acceptance.

In this section Justin and Alexis talk about their desire to learn more about themselves.

"See what great love the Father has lavished on us, that we should be called children of God! And that is what we are!"
(1 John 3:1)

God is love! So as we seek love, we are meant to be seeking God and understanding how we must operate in relation to Him.

STEP 1
PERSONAL NEED

This part of the personal needs sections discusses sexual trauma as Alexis unravels her experiences with abuse. Many abuse victims have had their perception altered due to abuse in their formative years. If you or someone you know has experienced similar abuse, we encourage you to process the following topics with caution as we challenge to process experiences that can impact our sense of worth, self-love, and self-care.

"Young, vulnerable [men and women] are often abused on a regular basis. As we enter adulthood, we carry these dark and frightening experiences that have altered us dramatically, shrinking our self-worth and ability to form meaningful and healthy relationships with others. We are scarcely aware of how profoundly changed we are, not just by the experiences themselves, but by the continuing burden of carrying the memory of them.

As children and teens, we internalize the crimes that have been committed against us and process it as shame, as though we have done something wrong, rather than having been wronged as tiny children. Almost inevitably, that child's shame expresses itself as toxic behavior when she becomes an adult. People who meet abused children as adults, acting out the worst of what they have learned, assume we are inherently toxic people, knowing nothing of what we have endured and how that shapes our behavior. Meanwhile, there is another

self, deep within: the real person, buried beneath that shame and heartache."
- Alexis

During this section, you will be challenged to uncover the "real you" buried underneath the abuse and traumatic experiences.

As Alexis shares her early years of experience with others using her body without her permission while being under age, how can you relate? Do you or friends of yours have similar experiences or stories? If so, how can you be an advocate to prevent others from experiencing similar trauma?

_____

_____

_____

_____

_____

As you think about your formative years of sex education, what beliefs about sex and intimacy do you feel you were taught?

_____

_____

_____

_____

_____

_____

What things did you find untrue? How have you learned and formed new ways of viewing your body and your own sexual experiences in a Godly way? Provide scriptures that have validated your point of view.

_____

_____

_____

_____

_____

_____

_____

_____

_____

What would you tell a younger version of yourself about sex now that you're living a Godly life? What are some of the pitfalls that you could have avoided?

_____

_____

_____

_____

_____

_____

_____

List a set of boundaries that you deem inappropriate when discussing consent. This can include, but is not limited to touching (name the specific areas), words said, and other boundaries you've set for yourself and others.

_____

_____

_____

_____

_____

_____

_____

_____

_____

_____

Alexis lost her mother by suicide at the age of six years old. Parents are fundamental in the development and growth of a child as they form their identity and meaning of love, compassion, and worthiness.

You may, or may not have experienced the loss of a parent, but in what ways upon reflection, do you feel abandoned by one of your parents as a child? What would you like to say to them today? In what ways do you feel they did not prepare you for how to handle life? In addition to this, what do you know about their family of origin and generational trauma?

Generational trauma is a traumatic event that began decades prior to the current generation and has impacted the way that individuals understand, cope with, and heal from trauma.

To learn more about trauma and different forms of trauma, please visit medicinenet.com and review the "What Are the 3 Types of Trauma?" article by Medical Author: Shaziya Allarakha, MD.

_____

_____

_____

_____

_____

_____

_____

_____

_____

_____

Alcohol usually plays a large role in the dysfunction of a family. What is your relationship with drugs or alcohol? How were drugs or alcohol used in your family's culture?

_____

_____

_____

_____

_____

"Every night, I would listen to "Imagine Me" by Kirk Franklin. I would play it after my dad was done with me, while wrapping my arms around my dog Jake's neck, crying into his marble black and white fur. It gave me hope. It made me feel safe. I heard this song one time when I went to church with a friend and held onto the lyrics…"

Imagine me
Loving what I see when the mirror looks at me 'cause I I imagine me
In a place of no insecurities
And I'm finally happy 'cause
I imagine me
Letting go of all of the ones who hurt me
'Cause they never did deserve me
Can you imagine me?
Saying no to thoughts that try to control me Remembering all you told me
Lord, can you imagine me?
Over what my mama said
And healed from what my daddy did
And I wanna live and not read that page again
Imagine me, being free, trusting you totally, finally I can Imagine me
I admit it was hard to see
You being in love with someone like me
But finally I can
Imagine me
Being strong
And not letting people break me down
You won't get that joy this time around
Can you imagine me
In a world (in a world) where nobody has to live afraid? Because of your love, fear's gone away
Can you imagine me?
Letting go of my past
And glad I have another chance

Imagine Me by Kirk Franklin

VISUAL PROJECT

Take a moment to think of the songs that may have helped get you through challenging times. What songs did you have on repeat? Take a moment to write your playlist here:

_____

_____

_____

_____

_____

_____

_____

If you remember the lyrics that carried you through your moments of struggle, write them in the space below:

_____

_____

_____

_____

_____

_____

_____

_____

_____

_____

_____

What scripture have helped you with overcoming trauma and understanding you experiences? Here are a few that have helped us become the person we are today:

"Consider it pure joy, my brothers and sisters, whenever you face trials of many kinds, because you know that the testing of your faith produces perseverance. Let perseverance finish its work so that you may be mature and complete, not lacking anything."
James 1:2-4 NIV

""Come to me, all you who are weary and burdened, and I will give you rest. Take my yoke upon you and learn from me, for I am gentle and humble in heart, and you will find rest for your souls. For my yoke is easy and my burden is light.""
Matthew 11:28-30 NIV

_____

_____

_____

_____

_____

_____

_____

_____

_____

_____

_____

_____

Can you imagine the compounding trauma of having to testify against your abuser and becoming a ward of the state at the same time? Can you relate to Alexis' story of how she entered foster care?

What coping strategies have you used to process your trauma? Do you believe these activities are helping you cope with your abuse? Why or why not?

_____

_____

_____

_____

_____

Have you ever feared telling the truth about your abuse because of what might happen? What would you do if a friend confided these things to you? How would you help others in this situation?

_____

_____

_____

For Alexis, school was her sacred space, the place she owned and that helped her make it through a very rough season. What is your safe place? Where do you run to and find solace for the journey?

_____

_____

_____

STEP 2
DISCOVERING IDENTITY

Have you analyzed the customs and practices of your family and community? Have the practices of your environment resulted in happiness and success for your peers and other family members?

In this section of the Identity chapter, we unpack Justin's experiences and identity as it relates to community and parental influences on character.

"Having strong parental figures instills self-confidence and a sense of worthiness. Good parents validate their child's sense of importance and recognize them as an individual with their own needs. They also guide by example, and in doing so, instill character in their kids, a firm understanding of right and wrong, and the sense of security they need to make mistakes and learn from them as they shape their consciences. And of course, parents are supposed to provide stability. I was only able to figure these things out later, backward, after taking stock of what I didn't have growing up. I never exactly felt loved by my parents and that's why I believe I've felt worthlessness throughout my life."
- Justin

VISUAL ACTIVITY

In the mirror below draw the things that you grew up around during your childhood and how it formed your own behavior and fundamental beliefs.

Who/what were your idols growing up? Who filled the role model gap for you?

_____

_____

_____

_____

_____

_____

_____

Parenting is hard. But when parents have addictions and poor coping skills it becomes harder on the entire family unit. Though you may, or may not have had drug addictions in your family or households, in what ways have you or other family members become dependent on things that are not fulfilling? In what ways can you relate to the struggles and family dynamics within Justin's household?

_____

_____

_____

_____

_____

_____

_____

_____

_____

"[Justin's mother]'s former coworker only stayed with us for a week, but she noticed the quality of life we were living. We were behind on rent for months and regularly without hot water and heat. The refrigerator was always empty until the first of the month when we received our food stamps. Hundreds of roaches would scatter in the bedrooms once you turned the light on. We lived with roaches, bed bugs, and any other thing you could think of. When my mom's drug addiction got worse with her new boyfriend, her former coworker truly saw us at our worst. One or two days after she left, Child Protective Services (CPS) came knocking on our door."
- Justin

Many of the adults in Alexis and Justin's lives suspected things were not good or healthy for the children. When you read about the coworker that stayed with Justin's family that might have made Child Protective Services aware of their situation, what feelings arise towards them? Did they do the right thing? Why or why not?

_____

_____

_____

_____

_____

_____

_____

_____

_____

_____

In what ways could there have been help and intervention prior to this point? What can you see as the needs of Justin and his siblings during this challenging time?

_____

_____

_____

_____

Have you ever had others make decisions for you, that at the time you couldn't understand why or see how those decisions would be better in the long run?

_____

_____

_____

Have you or anyone you know ever been homeless? Even if it is not under the same dire circumstances, consider times between selling your home and moving into a new one; a delay in an apartment being ready or having to be at the mercy of sleeping on a friend's couch. What are some things you missed by not having a safe and consistent space to call home?

_____

_____

_____

_____

Is there someone on your radar now that may be experiencing neglect or abuse? Hardship? What is God saying about the situation?

"God is our refuge and strength, an ever-present help in trouble." (Psalm 46:1b, NIV)

"I know that the Lord secures justice for the poor and upholds the cause of the needy." (Psalm 140:12)

"The Lord protects the foreigners among us. He cares for the orphans and widows, but he frustrates the plans of the wicked." (Psalm 146:9)

"He who oppresses the poor shows contempt for their Maker, but whoever is kind to the needy honors God." (Proverbs 14:31)

"If you help the poor, you are lending to the Lord—and he will repay you!" (Proverbs 19:17)

VISUAL ACTIVITY

In the two houses below choose one to represent how you grew up and one to represent the household you want to establish.

House of Origin

Who was in it (mother, father, siblings, others)? What were the feelings, moods and actions of its inhabitants? What did it feel like? What was the furniture and physical space like? On average how long did you stay at each home?

_____

_____

_____

_____

_____

_____

_____

_____

Last, do your best to describe the culture of the household/family.
Who established and contributed to it? What was your role within it?

_____

_____

_____

_____

_____

_____

_____

_____

_____

_____

_____

_____

_____

_____

_____

_____

_____

_____

_____

_____

House of Design

Who is in it? What are the moods and interactions of the people like? What do you want it to feel like? Where is it located? Don't be shy. Dream away!

_____

_____

_____

_____

_____

_____

_____

_____

_____

_____

_____

_____

Again, do your best to describe the culture. Who will be establishing and contributing to it? What is your role within it? What are the standards of the household?

_____

_____

_____

_____

When you look at the two houses, what are the similarities?

_____

_____

_____

What are the differences?

_____

_____

_____

What type of work will it take to go from the _Home of Origin_ to _Home by Design_? What new tools will you need?

_____

_____

_____

_____

_____

_____

DEFINITION OF COMMUNITY

Community is a gathering of people with shared principles and core values usually working towards similar goals for a particular area. Examples include, but are not limited to, church members, colleagues, business partners, coaches, tutors, teachers, and peers in the area.

Relying on others in the community is not complimentary but a must! Community members are contributors to your life. Be sure that your peers and closest friends are not a crutch or a barrier, but are actively pursuing goals alongside you. Everyone has a responsibility to the community and plays a role in one another's success or failure. Relationships should be mutually beneficial either spiritually, mentally, or emotionally.

Make a list of community resources, members, and opportunities that would make your dream home possible. Reflect on what was in your original home and the community that surrounded it. What elements contributed to the success or failure of your original household, and how the members in your new home can make the relationships in the community mutually beneficial.

_____

_____

_____

_____

_____

_____

_____

"You are the average of the five people you surround yourself with" -
Jim Rohn

Your Role in the Body of Christ

"Just as a body, though one, has many parts, but all its many parts
form one body, so it is with Christ."
1 Corinthians 12:12 NIV

For this section, we encourage you to read 1 Corinthians 12 to
understand the meaning and purpose of the Body of Christ. What
does it represent and what was God's purpose behind it?

_____

_____

_____

_____

_____

_____

What do you believe is your role in serving your community?

_____

_____

_____

_____

_____

_____

_____

When thinking about a team, a friend group, or network, surround yourself with people who are:

1. Strong in areas you are not
   "Carry each other's burdens, and in this way you will fulfill the law of Christ." Galatians 6:2 NIV

2. Challenge you to improve and grow
   "As iron sharpens iron, so one person sharpens another." Proverbs 27:17 NIV

3. Hold you responsible for mistakes and assist you in learning from them

"Brothers and sisters, if someone is caught in a sin, you who live by the Spirit should restore that person gently..." Galatians 6:1 NIV

Take the time to reflect on what your three to five core principles and values are. In addition to this, identify which are areas of potential growth. (Refer to page 137 for an example list).

Core Values

_____

_____

_____

_____

_____

Areas of Growth

_____

_____

_____

_____

_____

_____

Your circle should be a reflection of your foundational principles. The goal is to surround yourself with people who reflect your principles along with people who can support you with working on your areas of weakness. These people provide the courage to help you go above and beyond your capabilities.

Additional components of community include those serving in these areas (7 Life Domains from the Annie Casey Foundation):
1. Education and Academics
2. Finances and Employment
3. Housing
4. Physical and Mental Health
5. Social Relationships and Connections
6. Cultural and Personal Identity
7. Life Skills

Make a list of household, community members, and resources that support you or you are a part in these areas: (*If any of those areas were left blank, reflect on how you could seek out resources to fulfill that need.)

Education and Academics

_____   _____

_____   _____

_____   _____

_____   _____

Finances and Employment

_____   _____

_____   _____

_____   _____

_____   _____

Housing

_____   _____

_____   _____

_____   _____

_____   _____

Physical and Mental Health

_____   _____

_____   _____

_____   _____

_____   _____

Social Relationships and Connections

_____   _____

_____   _____

_____   _____

_____   _____

Cultural and Personal Identity

_____   _____

_____   _____

_____   _____

_____   _____

Life Skills

_____   _____

_____   _____

_____   _____

_____   _____

When thinking about how the body of the church can impact and
influence communities through these avenues, what approaches
come to mind? What programs and initiatives can churches and local
organizations create to focus on the categories above?

_____

_____

_____

_____

Even from a young age there were dreams and aspirations that were forming in Justin's heart about homes, rebuilding his city and thinking big. What things did you dream and ponder on as a child? What did your imagination see as possible?

_____

_____

_____

_____

_____

_____

_____

_____

_____

_____

_____

"As the Michigan winter began, I started shoveling snow to make a little money. Living in an abandoned house during the fall wasn't bad, but when winter came along, things weren't pretty. Detroit's winter winds are brutal. Living in a home with no heat became unbearable. Without running water, we had to scoop snow off of the ground, carry it inside in buckets and wait for it to melt to use as makeshift showers.

No one in the house had a bed so we regularly piled up clothes to sleep on to avoid feeling the wood and sharp nails sticking out of the floor.

We lived on baloney, peanut butter and jelly sandwiches, and anything we could make easily. To this day, the smell of gasoline recalls those gasoline heaters we used to warm our dinner in abandoned housing. My dad had been making excuses for months of why he couldn't fix the house and resorted to hiding from CPS. I began to lose faith in my parents. They told us that we would have the house fixed by the time CPS came to visit again. They never had any plans to fix the house at all, and my dreams of making it a home were long gone. I thought fixing the house would be the first piece of making us into one happy family. When CPS finally visited, our parents told us to hide. I ducked behind the living room couch in case they peaked through the windows. We all remained silent as we heard the social worker knock on the door."

- Justin

Have you lost faith in an adult in your life that along the way had their own issues and could not help you navigate yours? What did you do? Who are the people you can count on in your life today and how did you find these people?

_____

_____

_____

_____

_____

_____

_____

_____

Losing faith in the adults in your life is a hard thing. What decisions and choices could Justin's parents have made that would have kept him and his siblings safer, more protected? What resources and agencies do you know of that could have helped before it got to this point?

_____

_____

_____

_____

_____

_____

"We did our best, but my parents had no choice but to let us go. One month later, we entered foster care at the start of spring. As the youngest two boys of five siblings, my brother Khalil and I, at age 11 and nine, entered the foster care system together and journeyed through the system for years. Because he was two years older, he became my role model. Khalil played the role of a father figure and I mimicked his every move. We had an unbreakable bond up until we were separated at 17.

My sister Tiffany, 18, was preparing to start a family of her own. She gave birth to her first child that April. My 14-year-old brother Andre temporarily lived with my uncle for a few months. He always had a conflict in every home in which he was placed, making no living situation a viable long-term solution for him. Eventually he went AWOL.

All four of us separated on our individual journeys; it was up to us to figure out life on our own, with the foundation set by our parents. I still clung to the faith I'd had in my parents. At the same time, I felt that they had let me down completely. Here is where my issues with trust began. If I couldn't trust my parents, I reasoned, who would I be able to trust?"

- Justin

Have you ever been separated from a friend or loved one? What was the loss like for you? How did it impact your ability to form new bonds and secure relationships?

How is your faith and trust in God reflected by your experience trusting people? Are those two things connected? If so, should they be?

_____

_____

_____

_____

_____

_____

_____

_____

_____

_____

_____

_____

STEP 3
ACTION STEP

Write down a list of important resources available to you that would be valuable in the case of an emergency. Think government resources, non-profits, school employees, doctors, etc.

How can you reach them? Who would you choose to contact for what emergency?

_____

_____

_____

_____

_____

_____

_____

_____

_____

_____

_____

_____

_____

_____

Definition of Love

Based on Redefining Normal Definition of Love:
"Sell-out" | "The Cycle" | "Turning Point"

SESSION AIM:

Understanding feelings surrounding the idea of love. Thinking critically about complex relationships.

Everyone has their own idea and definition of love. Most people's definitions have been shaped by others and or developed upon an unhealthy foundation. Reflect on the steps Alexis and Justin had to take to change the trajectory of their path and their definition of love, along with the expectations of their romantic and familial relationships.

"Our parents set the foundation and standard for love. We learn how to love and receive love from them. But if parents are unaware of what healthy love is themselves, it is inevitable for children to unconsciously inherit destructive habits and patterns from their parents.

This cycle allows people that are unfamiliar with a healthy definition of love to define what love is for generations to come. Because family plays such an intimate role in shaping our values, morals, and habits, consequently, they can harm us the most. Most adults spend their entire lives healing from their childhood and yearning for love, acceptance, and praise that wasn't provided by their parents."
- Alexis

STEP 1
PERSONAL NEED

VISUAL ACTIVITY

Mandala Heart coloring can be therapeutic. It is a way for us to create, and yet have free space in our brains to think through things without stopping our thought processes. Below you will find a beautiful heart mandala.

For each portion of the verse on the next page, we have attached a coordinating color to use while meditating on that portion of the Scripture. Work on one color at a time while you continue to ruminate on that portion. By the end, you will have created a meaningful and vibrant depiction of the beauty and complexity of true love.

1 Corinthians 13:4-7 (list version used below)

Yellow: Love is patient.

Light green: Love is kind.

Light blue: Love endures with patience and serenity.

Light Red: Love is kind and thoughtful.

Green: It is not jealous or envious.

Orange: Love does not brag and is not proud or arrogant.

Purple: It is not rude; it is not self-seeking.

Red: It is not provoked [nor overly sensitive and easily angered].

Black: It does not keep a record of wrong.

Yellow: It does not rejoice at injustice, but rejoices with the truth [when right and truth prevail].

ACTION STEPS TO LOVE

1. Start with displaying these action steps for yourself and then display them for others

2. True leadership starts with self-love. You can only lead/love people in ways that you've done for yourself

Our partners can't fix us, just as we cannot fix them. We can't fully love someone without loving ourselves first.

Reflect on the definition of love that was shaped for you as a child and/or teenager. Is your definition different now? Describe your definition of love below.

_____

_____

_____

_____

_____

How do you display this definition of love for yourself and others?

_____

_____

_____

_____

_____

_____

Justin: Trauma can be passed down as a culture and normalized within a family.

1. _____

2. _____

3. _____

How do you and your family face reality or alternatively protect the unspoken reality of your family history?

_____

_____

_____

_____

_____

_____

Justin and Alexis often bottled up their emotions, unwilling to share their hardships with others. Ensuring that you have a support system that allows you to process your emotions healthily, make a list below of 3-4 people you feel you could discuss your hardships, trauma, and shortcomings with.

Are they willing to listen and understand how you feel without disregarding your words? Are they showing empathy or sympathy? Do they offer more "I" statements or "You" statements?

Ex: Sympathetic statement: "I'm sorry for your loss, I understand where you're coming from."

Vs

Empathetic statement: *"Can you tell me more about how you feel? Can you tell me how I can help?"*

As you list your support system, consider these examples above.

1. _____

2. _____

3. _____

4. _____

In what ways can you work on being more empathetic in your own life? When it comes to embracing those of other races, political point of views, education levels, etc. How often are you willing to listen and learn as opposite to enforce your beliefs? Consider *Luke 10:25-37* in your answer.

_____

_____

_____

_____

_____

_____

_____

_____

_____

_____

STEP 2
GROUP DISCUSSION

"Unresolved trauma can easily be passed down from generation to generation. Trauma can be passed down as culture and normalized within a family. The reason it remains within a family for so long is because it is often unidentified and then mislabeled. Multiple families have labeled their unresolved trauma as love. When you identify trauma as love, you then accept everything that comes with it."
- Justin

What is your emotional reaction to this statement? What are some of the experiences in your youth that created a false sense of what was normal? Where would you say you are in the process of redefining what your new normal will be? Who has helped you through that learning curve?

_____

_____

_____

_____

_____

_____

_____

_____

_____

_____

To know your ACEs score, search 'NPR ACEs Quiz' and take the test.

What was your score? Was it high or low? Are you surprised? What is some other information you read on the website that helps you understand Justin and Alexis, yourself, or people served in the foster care community?

_____

_____

_____

_____

_____

_____

When you think about the area you grew up in as a child, what/who was in the one-mile radius around your home?

_____

_____

_____

_____

_____

_____

_____

_____

Take a moment to share with your group what your radius was like using some of the markers that Justin and Alexis alluded to:

- What was the physical environment like? (City, country, rural, suburban)
- Socio-economic make up of the area? Was it upper class, middle class, mixed class, blue collar?
- What was the feel and make-up of your neighborhood and neighbors? (Fun, loud, quiet, reserved, friendly, etc)
- School and educational quality and access?
- Community resources (Churches, libraries, grocery stores, daycares, banks, etc.)

Upon further reflection, do you see a correlation and/or connection to the opportunities you have and/or lifestyle you live now?

_____

_____

_____

_____

_____

_____

_____

_____

_____

_____

_____

How would you define "Internal Locus of Control" as mentioned in the book but in your own words? Locus of control is the degree to which people believe that they, as opposed to external forces, have control over the outcome of events in their lives.

_____

_____

_____

_____

_____

_____

_____

_____

How much influence do you believe external forces have in your life?

_____

_____

_____

_____

_____

_____

_____

_____

_____

_____

Our lives were on a certain trajectory of abuse, neglect, and brokenness but we had to fight through the millions of hurdles and societal expectations to become who we are today.

LOCUS OF CONTROL

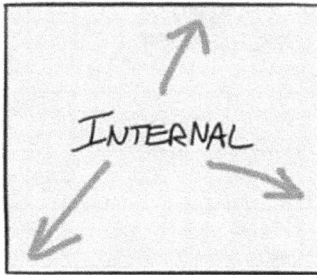

You Determine Your Fate

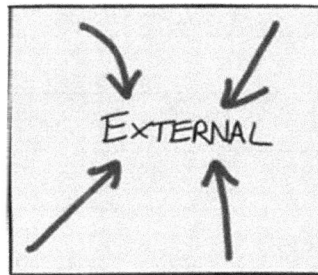

Your Life Happens To You, Rather Than Due To You

Image from www.cedarcolorado.org

We believe that in many circumstances, our own actions determine the rewards we obtain (internal locus of control), but our parents and so many other people in our lives believe that their own behavior doesn't matter much and that what happens to them is generally outside of their control (external locus of control).

Can you name a situation where your "locus of control" was put to the test and you utilized it to create your own success? Also, name a time in the past where you felt that the control and power for the specific situation remained outside of your control. What was your reaction to it and how could you have adjusted your reaction for a better outcome?

_____

_____

_____

_____

_____

_____

_____

_____

_____

_____

_____

_____

_____

_____

_____

_____

_____

_____

STEP 3
ACTION STEP

Brainstorm a list of physical places that you go to when you feel that you've lost control. What qualities do these places have in common? What are other places that could be considered a "safe space"?

1. _____

2. _____

3. _____

What words, thoughts, or Scriptures come to you while in this place? What do you feel that God is communicating to you?

_____

_____

_____

_____

_____

_____

_____

_____

_____

_____

_____

_____

_____

Breaking Cycles
Part 1

Based on Redefining Normal Breaking Cycles Part 1:
"Revealing the Truth in My Trauma" | "Vulnerable Through the Pain"
"Mental Warfare" | "True Colors" | "Self-Sabotage" | "Image"

SESSION AIM:

Understanding the root of trauma and the root it has on our future.

"Never get so comfortable in pain that you forget
happiness is an option." - Anonymous

What the Statistics Say:
1 in 6 U.S. adults live with a mental illness, equating
to almost 43.8 million adults

Black children have the highest rate of suicide deaths within children
ages 5 to 11. Suicide is ranked as the third leading cause of death for
Black men ages 15-24

STARTER QUESTION

List the positive role models and people you were influenced by during three particular parts of your life that showed you a better way of living, a different way of doing life?:

Childhood (infancy to 12 years) - _____

Teen Years (13 to 18 years) - _____

Young Adult (19 - 30 years) - _____

When you experienced something traumatic, what beliefs about your responsibility or "your part" did you start to own?
In retrospect, with what you are currently learning about trauma, do you view these situations any differently? Why or why not?

_____

_____

_____

_____

_____

_____

_____

_____

_____

_____

_____

Gaslighting: Alexis's counselor defined the term as "someone's actions that intentionally make you feel crazy, causing you to second guess yourself, and your values." Go online and read the working definition and a few articles that you can find about abuse and gaslighting.

_____

_____

_____

_____

_____

Have you experienced any of this personally?

_____

_____

_____

_____

_____

_____

_____

_____

_____

_____

_____

_____

_____

Escalation of Commitment: We have the tendency to _____ to _____ in something even though it's been years and we have seen no _____.

"I expected love to hurt. That's the only form of love I've ever known"
- Alexis

From your childhood experiences, did you expect the same thing from love or something different? Explain:

_____

_____

_____

_____

_____

_____

_____

_____

_____

_____

_____

_____

_____

_____

_____

_____

STEP 1
PERSONAL NEED

"At the end of the day: hurt people, hurt people.
Healed people, heal people."

A part of Alexis' personal narrative includes healing from sexual trauma and abuse.

When you read this quote, what camp are you in? Healing or Hurting? How do you move to the healing side? Explain how you are working to heal people from traumatizing experiences by evaluating your own behavior.

_____

_____

_____

_____

_____

What are some messages about sexual intimacy and relationships that you have received? What experiences have distorted your view of sexual intimacy and the purpose which God created?

_____

_____

_____

_____

What was your "sex talk" as a teen or child? Was it from a parent, teacher, mentor, family member, etc.?

_____

_____

_____

_____

There was a strong connection to pornography or sexual acts and shame for Justin. How have you navigated your emotions surrounding early exposure to sex?

_____

_____

_____

_____

What desires and decisions did Justin form about his views on protecting and caring for women? Where did he learn these things?

_____

_____

_____

_____

_____

_____

_____

_____

When thinking about the growth and development of family, how can we teach our loved ones about God's perspective of sex and intimacy in a healthy way? How do we avoid passing along negative or ungodly perspectives of sex onto the people we love based upon our potential sexual trauma?

_____

_____

_____

_____

When you think of your family of origin, what goals did you have for forming a life and family of your own? Were you positively or negatively impacted by the example you were given?

_____

_____

_____

_____

What impact does domestic violence have on a child witnessing it? How has it impacted you or your network of friends and family?

_____

_____

_____

_____

_____

_____

Can you name the different forms of domestic violence beyond physical? Feel free to provide examples.

_____

_____

_____

_____

"I had never been taught the rules of regular, functioning households. Instead I had grown up in an almost lawless environment, where survival was the only concern." - Justin

What would you consider to be "normative" rules for a functioning household? Make a list below:

_____

_____

_____

_____

_____

_____

_____

_____

_____

_____

_____

_____

Have you ever come to the point of asking or wanting to ask:

- Why was this normal and acceptable in our family?
- At what point do we discuss these issues and resolve them for a healthy and prosperous future?

When you read about Justin's experience, the violent trauma of Justin being assaulted and losing six teeth, what experiences can you equate it to? What significant traumatizing things happened in the "help and care" that were hurtful instead of helpful?

_____

_____

_____

_____

_____

_____

_____

_____

_____

_____

_____

_____

_____

_____

"What happens when you've met your life partner, but you still have unprocessed and unresolved trauma from your past?"

Talk about a time your traumatic experiences kept you from developing a relationship. This could include a friendship, professional relationship, or romantic partner.

_____

_____

_____

_____

_____

_____

"It never seemed to occur to anyone that it was more than my face that needed to recover..." - Justin

Even though society is more aware of invisible illnesses, most of the time, it is still difficult to recognize in ourselves and others. What were some of the holistic care points that were not addressed in your life?

On a daily/weekly basis, reflect on where you are in the areas below. Using a scale of 1-10, rate yourself.
1 =unstable and loss complete control
10 = healthy, active, and maintaining stability
Describe why you rated your status as you did.

Physical: _____

_____

_____

_____

_____

Emotional: _____

_____

_____

_____

_____

Social: _____

_____

_____

_____

_____

Relational: _____

_____

_____

_____

_____

_____

Spiritual: _____

_____

_____

_____

_____

Mental: _____

_____

_____

_____

_____

We encourage you to find an accountability partner to discuss your stability in these areas. Check-in with them on a biweekly basis, at the very least, to ensure that you are actively prioritizing your needs and self-care. If you are below a five or six in any of these areas, please check with a trusted adult for guidance and support.

Go online to find a reputable psychological or medical site and find the working biological, mental and emotional experience of an anxiety attack.

Here are our suggestions:
https://www.psychologytoday.com
https://www.verywellhealth.com

_____

_____

_____

_____

_____

Have you or someone close to you experienced an anxiety attack? What was it like?

_____

_____

_____

_____

When you think of the generational history of both Alexis' mom and grandmother dying from suicide, what key influences have helped her overcome her daunting odds?

_____

_____

_____

_____

_____

_____

_____

_____

IMAGO

"In a relationship with someone who's gone through extremely traumatic experiences, I needed to support her individual growth. Not for the relationship, but for her betterment as a woman... Your parental figures can either save you from a life of difficulties or provoke a reckoning with the pain and trauma they've caused in your life.

Parents are the tree of the family. When choosing your partner, you are deciding what type of fruit you would like to produce. Are you going to produce good fruit that your children can consume for a lifetime or toxic fruit from which your children will be poisoned? If that trauma is unaddressed, the poison can seep down into many generations.

The fruit in this analogy represents culture, identity, and ideology. Some parents create a family culture in which kids thrive while others are unable or unwilling to do so, and many children suffer greatly as a result." - Justin

But the fruit of the Spirit is love, joy, peace, patience, kindness, goodness, faithfulness, gentleness, and self-control. Galatians 5:22-23

What expectations did Justin and Alexis have together facing their individual trauma and working on it individually and together?

_____

_____

_____

_____

_____

What triggers do you bring with you in your relationships?

_____

_____

_____

_____

_____

How well do you know your body? What signs are showing when you need to seek out help from a medical or other professional to work through stress, anxiety and depression?

_____

_____

_____

_____

_____

_____

_____

_____

_____

_____

_____

_____

_____

_____

What limitations do certain communities and their youth face in regards to access (Physical, emotional, social, relational, spiritual, and mental resources that contribute to growth and stability), awareness and resources to deal with the challenges of the community itself?

Access meaning physical, emotional, social, relational, spiritual, and mental resource that contribute to growth and stability.

Ex: Low-income communities, Middle-income communities, Higher-income communities.
(higher-income communities may have access to many things, but may not be AWARE that they have trauma cycles playing out and they too may need help/intervention).

_____

_____

_____

_____

_____

In what ways can a church family support in their struggle?

_____

_____

_____

_____

_____

_____

What has been your experience in counseling or therapy? What do yo believe makes a therapist a good fit? When do you feel you made the most progress?

_____

_____

_____

_____

_____

WHAT YOU NEED TO CONSIDER
WHEN LOOKING FOR COUNSELING

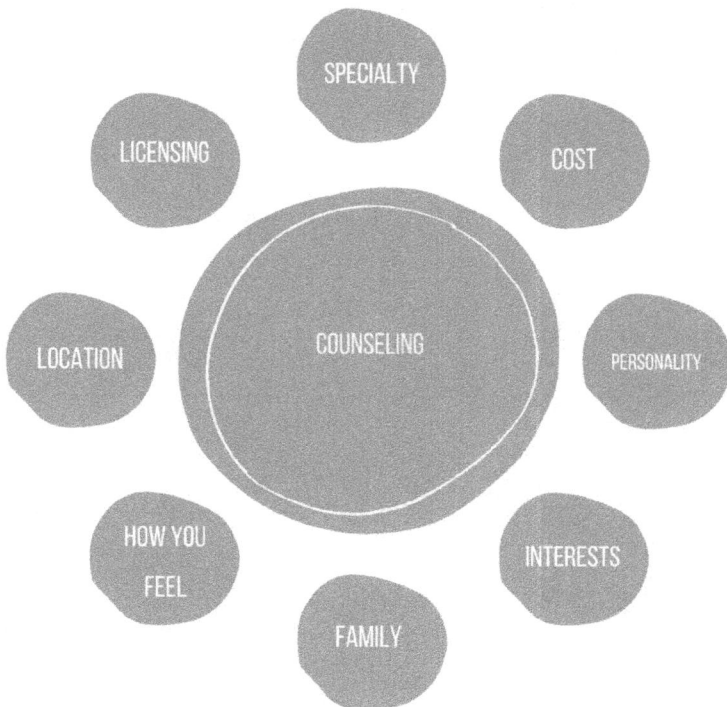

SPECIALTY

LICENSING

COST

LOCATION

COUNSELING

PERSONALITY

HOW YOU FEEL

FAMILY

INTERESTS

Addiction has been generational for many families. In order for us to support ourselves, our family, and other people we must define what addiction is and work to a more healthy solution.

DEFINITION OF ADDICTION
(ACCORDING TO MERRIAM-WEBSTER)

a compulsive, chronic, physiological or psychological need for a habit-forming substance, behavior, or activity having harmful physical, psychological, or social effects and typically causing well-defined symptoms (such as anxiety, irritability, tremors, or nausea) upon withdrawal or abstinence : the state of being addicted.

What truths from your experience growing up have you neglected to share or have discussions about because of protecting your family's image?

_____

_____

_____

_____

_____

_____

_____

_____

_____

_____

It was my responsibility to stop _____ my childhood trauma and to start seeing it as separate from my God-given value.

If you know someone who has experienced trauma, what services and needs are unique to them? This will help develop a holistic plan of success.

_____

_____

_____

_____

_____

_____

_____

_____

_____

_____

_____

_____

_____

_____

_____

_____

_____

I learned I had to be _____ and _____ with myself before I could commit to another person.

STEP 2
GROUP DISCUSSION

Take time to read through the following belief statements. Which ones would you agree with? Which ones do you not agree with? Now share within the Facebook group times or situations throughout this book that you could see these beliefs forming or share about your own experience.

- I am treated badly, therefore I am bad.
- I am at fault, it's my job to fix it.
- If I am at odds with my parents, I have no power to change the dynamic.

Now that you have had the time to discuss, take a moment to rewrite these statements to be more reflective of a person who truly values themselves and not just their relationships.

Take your "How healthy is my relationship?" quiz available at re-definingnormal.com

REDEFINING NORMAL

How Healthy Is My Relationship?

Following are two lists, one of healthy relationship characteristics and one of unhealthy traits. Many relationships have a combination of both. The point of this exercise is to figure out what things in your relationship are healthy or unhealthy, so you can gain appreciation for the best things and decide what you want to change. Read both lists, and check the box next to every statement that is true about your relationship.

I am evaluating my relationship with: _____

IS IT HEALTHY?

Check the box if you and this person....

- ○ Have fun together more often than not
- ○ Each enjoy spending time separately, with your own friends, as well as with each other's friends
- ○ Always feel safe with each other
- ○ Trust each other
- ○ Are faithful to each other if you have made this commitment
- ○ Support each other's individual goals in life, like getting a job or going to college
- ○ Respect each other's opinions, even when they are different
- ○ Solve conflicts without putting each other down, cursing at each other or making threats
- ○ Both accept responsibility for your actions
- ○ Both apologize when you're wrong
- ○ Have equal decision-making power about what you do in your relationship
- ○ Each control your own money
- ○ Are proud to be with each other
- ○ Encourage each other's interests - like sports and extracurricular activities
- ○ Have some privacy - your letters, diary, personal phone calls are respected as your own
- ○ Have close friends & family who like the other person and are happy about your relationship
- ○ Never feel like you're being pressured for sex
- ○ Communicate about sex, if your relationship is sexual
- ○ Allow each other 'space' when you need it
- ○ Always treat each other with respect

IS IT UNHEALTHY?

Check the box if you and this person....

- ○ Gets extremely jealous or accuses the other of cheating
- ○ Puts the other down by calling names, cursing or making the other feel bad about him or herself
- ○ Yells at and treats the other like a child
- ○ Doesn't take the other person, or things that are important to him/her, seriously
- ○ Doesn't listen when the other talks
- ○ Frequently criticizes the other's friends or family
- ○ Pressures the other for sex, or makes sex hurt or feel humiliating
- ○ Has ever threatened to hurt the other or commit suicide if they leave
- ○ Cheats or threatens to cheat
- ○ Tells the other how to dress
- ○ Has ever grabbed, pushed, hit, or physically hurt the other
- ○ Blames the other for your own behavior ("If you hadn't made me mad, I wouldn't have...")
- ○ Embarrasses or humiliates the other
- ○ Smashes, throws or destroys things
- ○ Tries to keep the other from having a job or furthering his/her education
- ○ Makes all the decisions about what the two of you do
- ○ Tries to make the other feel crazy or plays mind games
- ○ Goes back on promises
- ○ Acts controlling or possessive - like you own your partner
- ○ Uses alcohol or drugs as an excuse for hurtful behavior
- ○ Ignores or withholds affection as a way of punishing the other
- ○ Depends completely on the other to meet social or emotional needs

This list is a way of identifying some of the healthy and unhealthy characteristics of your relationship - it does not cover every possible situation. You may want to share this list with someone in your support system, and talk about where you want to make changes in your relationship and how you can begin to do this.

Based off Wellness Reproduction and Publishing Worksheet

How did receiving a planner and being teachable help Justin go from overwhelmed and failing to finding success in more than just school?

_____

_____

_____

_____

How did a lack of support system and parental involvement thread its way through Justin's story? How have your parents' involvement or lack there of impacted your story?

_____

_____

_____

_____

According to psychcentral.com's Here Is How to Identify Your Attachment Style article.

- Signs of a secure attachment style include:
- ability to regulate your emotions
- easily trusting others
- effective communication skills
- ability to seek emotional support
- comfortable being alone
- comfortable in close relationships
- ability to self-reflect in partnerships
- being easy to connect with

- ability to manage conflict well
- high self-esteem
- ability to be emotionally available

What happens when that is not felt and internalized by children?

_____

_____

_____

_____

_____

_____

Youth have a peer group and identify with interests, hobbies, or activities that may differ from those of the parent. Youth are able to seek help when they encounter a challenge. Youth may become distressed, angry, or sad, but is able to use support(s) of friends, family, teachers, coaches, and/or a therapist to recover, and resumes typical activities.
(Bowlby, 1982, Cooper, et al., 2016)

"I felt worthless and still not good enough to be loved" - If you could write a short message to college Justin to help him work through the belief statement above, what would you include?

_____

_____

_____

_____

BOUNDARIES

"Every single relationship with friends, family, and colleagues has boundaries, we just have to decide for ourselves what the parameters are in order to protect ourselves. Depending on the relationship, we can be taken advantage of, compromise beliefs, and be sucked dry financially, emotionally, mentally, and spiritually." - Alexis

How would you define what a boundary is in a relationship? Describe the boundaries you have had to establish with certain people in your life and past.

_____

_____

_____

_____

_____

_____

_____

_____

_____

_____

_____

_____

_____

_____

_____

_____

HOLIDAYS

What holidays did your family of origin celebrate? Share with your group what things went well and what didn't.

_____

_____

_____

_____

Do the holidays trigger past memories or motives that have been exposed through actions of family and friends?

_____

_____

_____

_____

What changes and boundaries did Justin develop after coming to the awakening that "the burden of wanting their love was killing me"? Have you ever come to a similar place or experience that makes you question what love looks like and what boundaries are needed?

_____

_____

_____

_____

_____

BUILDING ROMANTIC RELATIONSHIPS

What is the difference between dating casually, being a serial girlfriend/boyfriend/partner, or a marriage focus?

_____

_____

_____

_____

What is your criteria or "must haves" in your ideal partner?

_____

_____

_____

_____

What would it mean for you to find a worthy life partner/spouse?

_____

_____

_____

_____

What would it look like for you to date someone with matching values?

_____

_____

_____

_____

What kind of person do you want to be when you meet your future mate?

_____

_____

_____

_____

Even if you are in a relationship use the T-Chart below and list what you need and want from a partner. Use this as a time of reflection of what you, too, could offer your current partner that would help open new discussions of felt needs and expectations moving forward.

Want	Need

Dating with a purpose of finding or being found by your future life partner (Prov. 18:22). What would that look like for you?

_____

_____

_____

_____

_____

_____

_____

_____

_____

_____

_____

_____

_____

_____

_____

_____

_____

_____

_____

_____

STEP 3
ACTION STEP

Love Languages Quiz and Exploration
Visit 5lovelanguages.com to take your love language test

Example:
If I (worked on my relationship with my parents/spent more time in counseling/understood my purpose) I would have what I need to build a successful relationship.

I want my relationship to be (filled with respect) where we could (appreciate, contribute, and serve) one another through our struggles.

Men/women commonly accept the role of (leadership) without developing the necessary (characteristics to do so).

_____

_____

_____

_____

_____

_____

_____

_____

_____

ACTIVITY

"Within the context of marriage, leadership means serving my partner in a manner she sees fit." - Justin. How is this similar or different from what you experience or believe? Is this a healthy statement?

_____

_____

_____

You are welcome to fill in the blanks with your own words or from the example.

If I _____, I would have what I need to build a successful relationship. .

I want my relationship to be _____ where we could _____, _____, _____ for another through our struggles.

Men/women commonly accept the role of a _____ without developing the necessary _____.

"Within the context of marriage, leadership means serving my partner in a manner she/he sees fit." How is this similar or different from what you experience or believe? Is this a healthy statement?

My role in marriage is to be a _____ type of partner. I expect my partner to _____ for me and our family.

In what ways has "play your role" been used to demean, control or limit you in a relationship?

_____

_____

_____

_____

_____

_____

_____

_____

_____

_____

What were some defining moments in your own life and journey that helped you clarify what you were going to be passionate about and pursue?

_____

_____

_____

_____

_____

_____

VISUAL ACTIVITY

If you have a chance to speak at an event about what you have learned from your experiences in life, what would you say? List some of the core beliefs and things you know need to change or that would have helped you through your dark times.

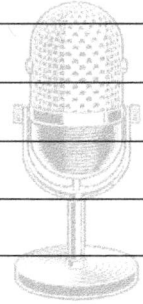

_____

_____

_____

_____

_____

_____

_____

_____

_____

_____

_____

_____

_____

_____

_____

_____

Breaking Cycles
Part 2

Based on Redefining Normal Breaking Cycles Part 2:
"Sacrifice & Submission" | "Talk it Out" | "City Kids Travel the Globe"
"The Proposal" | "Love is Not Always Black & White"

SESSION AIM:

Understanding perspectives of ourselves

"Breaking generational cycles can be a lonely, wrenching process. Children generally accept the practices of their family without question; looking back and questioning them later requires a determination stronger than the pain of separating from the only values they have ever known.

For many people, choosing to leave their environment to do better comes with being shunned or shamed by one's family. Children are sponges; they soak up messages from the moment they are born. Ways of thinking and communication (and ways of behaving in general) become deeply ingrained in our formative years. The social world we grow up in defines for us what's normal, acceptable, and praiseworthy." - Justin

It's easy to think this way as a child until you learn about Adverse Childhood Experiences (ACEs). These have a tremendous impact on future violence, victimization and perpetration, and lifelong health and opportunity. An ACE score (0 to 10) is a tally of different types of abuse, neglect, and other hallmarks of a rough childhood. According to the Adverse Childhood Experiences Study, the rougher your childhood, the higher your score is likely to be and the higher your risk for later health problems such as alcoholism, obesity, drug use, depression, suicide attempts, cancer, heart disease, and more." - Justin

STARTER QUESTION

What type of fruit would you like to produce?
(Fruit meaning the results you expect based upon the process and the work you put forth). What things would you expect to see in your future?
Emotional - Social - Cognitive - Educational- Spiritual - Relational - Financial

---

Justin used a time of physical distancing in their relationship (due to Alexis being in DC) to focus on his journey. "It was the last time to fight a battle I had postponed for nearly two decades."

If you were isolated from distractions and were forced to face issues you had been avoiding, what issues would you have to face?

STEP 1
PERSONAL NEED

I see a relationship as two individuals _____ happening side by side, in which both parties share _____ and _____ along with _____ and _____.

"I decided to use my acceptance of addiction as a source of power that no one could hold against me while I overcome the obstacles that were set before me." - Justin

What experiences have you had to redefine in order to overcome obstacles in a positive way?

_____

_____

_____

_____

_____

Alexis' adoptive parents Kim and Brian were influential to the healing journey for both Justin and Alexis. Have you experienced people like that or are you currently that person for someone else?

_____

_____

_____

_____

What were the boundaries and components to those relationships that made them work?

_____

_____

_____

_____

During the pandemic, Justin and Alexis lived with Alexis' parents, Kim and Brian. What amount of vulnerability would it take for you to serve others in ways that are sacrificial for your comfort?

_____

_____

_____

_____

How difficult would it be for you as a young person to open up and ask for mentorship and access to a couple you admire?

_____

_____

_____

_____

_____

_____

_____

_____

VISUAL ACTIVITY

On the image, labeled PRIVATE, write the things that you know about yourself and who you are when you are not looking to fit in with others.

Private   **Public**

 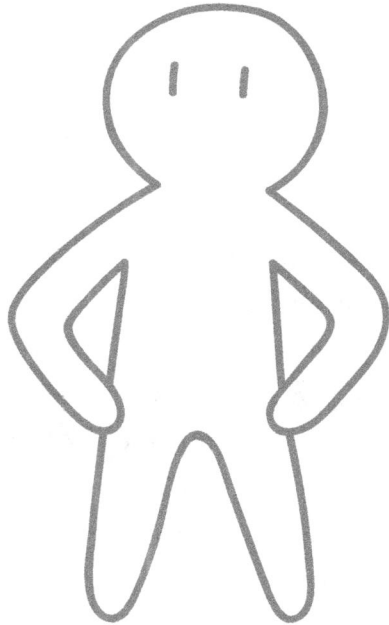

On the second image, labeled PUBLIC, write words that you feel describe who you have to be around others. What roles, images, actions do you tend to put on?

STEP 2
GROUP DISCUSSION

What are some communication strategies Justin and Alexis learned to implement into their communication guide as a couple? Discuss them as a group and write at least five in the spaces below.

_____

_____

_____

_____

"Traveling made us feel like we were taking on the world together. There was something powerful about getting on a plane and flying somewhere far away from the backdrop of what we'd grown up with, taking life into our own hands. This was the physical embodiment of the emotional journey we had taken together. When I was little, I couldn't just walk out and escape but, as adults, we were giving ourselves the power not only to leave, but to choose where we went."
- Alexis

When you reflect on this quote, what parts speak to your journey; what parts speak to how you help others work through theirs?

_____

_____

_____

_____

As Alexis began traveling abroad, what were some of the key elements that allowed her to gain new perspectives and develop a truer sense of self?

"I want to travel because of_____. I believe it will offer _____ for me, helping me _____ my future. "
Alexis shares how the lyrics from the Kirk Franklin song from her childhood had come full circle and redeemed. Do you have a similar experience? How have fears and hurt from your childhood been redeemed or restored? Describe some of these moments.

_____

_____

_____

_____

What things have you feared in the past and how did you overcome that fear? Moving, asking someone out, buying your first car, finding a job, traveling, going away from home for the first time?

_____

_____

_____

_____

_____

_____

_____

_____

SESSION AIM:

Visualizing your future, thinking about past relationships. How to build a foundation of success.

In this chapter Justin and Alexis talk about their experiences and how thankful they are for where they've ended up. They talk about how the values they've learned have led them to where they are.

40 - 50% of marriages end in divorce. The leading causes are infidelity, finances, and family conflict.

Around 70% of child poverty occurs in single-parent families. Children in single-parent homes are about five times more likely to be poor than children in married-couple homes, showing that family structure is the most important factor in predicting the upward social mobility of children.

STARTER QUESTION

From an evening of engagement bliss to a morning of attack and discouragement. How would you have handled the highs and lows? What parts of Justin and Alexis' healing journey gave them the tools to navigate moments of despair?

_____

_____

_____

_____

_____

Describe a time where you made a life altering decision that family and friends disagreed with? Did they offer reasonable advice and guidance? Did you consider their perspective? Please explain the situation as well as the end result and what could have been done better on both sides.

_____

_____

_____

_____

_____

_____

_____

_____

_____

STEP 1
PERSONAL NEED

Because each person is a product of two cultures, the relationship could be heading for a crash course. How can a couple be more intentional when building a relationship and finding agreement on which cultural values they'll continue practicing?

Example: Conversations around which practices can help or hurt the relationship, seeing which cultural practices work once acted upon, etc.

_____

_____

_____

_____

_____

Who would you (or did you) involve in the process of discernment regarding who and when to date.

Who would you (or did you) seek wisdom from or permission from before you propose(d)?

_____

_____

_____

_____

VISUAL ACTIVITY

Building blocks of success. In the stacked blocks below, use the open space to write different aspects of what "success" would look like for you. What things come first? What things are you still building and hoping for?

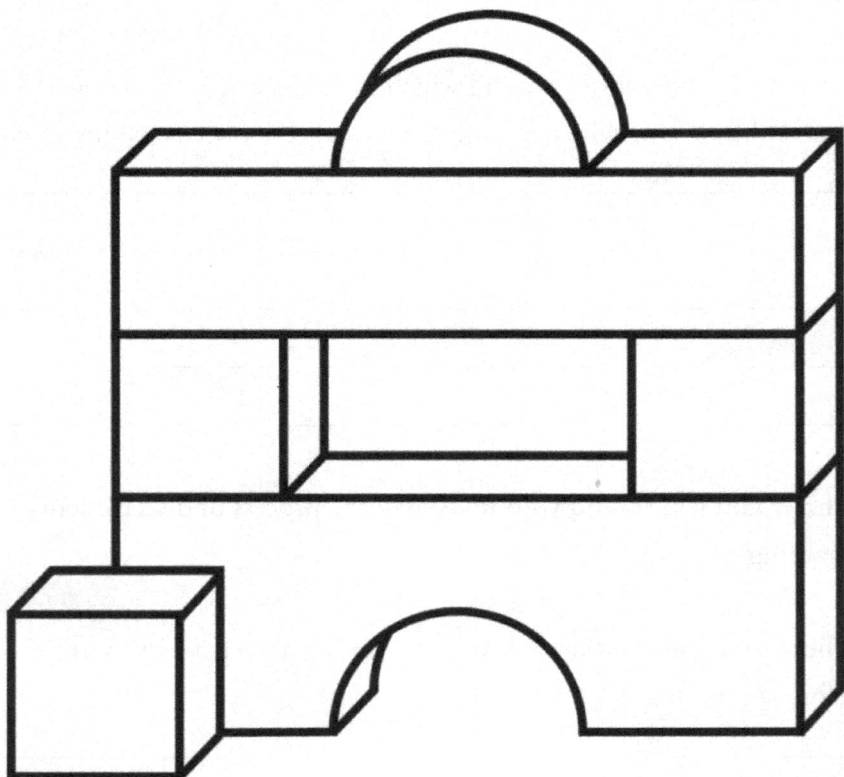

After you fill in all the blocks, take a look. What will you leave behind in the world? Will these blocks remain standing? Will they be useful to future generations? Will they stand firm against the stress of life, kids, marriage, relationships, job changes, etc. Why or why not?

_____

_____

_____

_____

_____

_____

_____

_____

_____

_____

_____

_____

_____

_____

_____

_____

_____

_____

_____

_____

_____

DEFINITION OF FAMILY

"Family plays the most intimate role in shaping our values, morals, and habits; consequently, it can harm us the most. We had to reflect on if the culture of our family set us on a path of success or failure."
- Justin

What are the characteristics of family?
Families most of the time are your biggest support system. In many situations, people need to have a definition of family beyond biological. This includes kinship, foster, adoptive, and traditional, etc.

1. **Selflessness**
   Making sure to serve others and making sacrifices

2. **Unconditional Love and Support**
   Supportive of in moments of need

3. **Properly resolving conflicts with communication**
   No gossip, violence, or avoidance when tackling issues

"Family supports you during your moments of sorrow, as well as joyfully celebrating your successes. Family is truthful and patient and sees the very best in you. Envy, bitterness, and resentment are not routine states in a healthy family. Peace, respect, and compromise are instead its organizing principles. I will no longer allow someone else's pain or damage to influence my identity."
- Justin

STEP 2
GROUP DISCUSSION

Have you ever had something that was extremely important to you but your family and/or friends ignored, made fun of, or denied its validity? How did you handle the pain, shame, or frustration of it?

_____

_____

_____

_____

If you could go back and have a conversation with the child you were at the age of trauma, what would you tell yourself? What would you tell them was possible?

_____

_____

_____

_____

What does it mean to you to "outgrow" a friendship? Would this be challenging for you to admit? Have you ever been in a place that you have experienced someone moving on or ahead without you? How did that feel?

_____

_____

_____

We are not a product of our _____ choices — we are
instead _____ by our own decisions.

What decisions are you currently sorting through? What decisions will
take you closer to your dreams? What decisions will take you farther
from your values?

_____

_____

_____

_____

_____

_____

_____

What changes in a relationship when transitioning from dating, then
to engagement, and then to marriage? How does that change the
responsibility and treatment of yourself and your spouse?

_____

_____

_____

_____

_____

_____

_____

We are designed to be _____, not _____.
Partner up with someone in your group and define what these two
words mean. Give examples of what that could look like in dating,
engagement, and marriage.

_____

_____

_____

_____

_____

_____

_____

_____

_____

_____

_____

_____

_____

_____

_____

_____

_____

_____

_____

ACTION STEPS TO FORGIVENESS

"We have experienced compounded trauma and are going through the process of daily growth and development. One of the biggest barriers standing in our way to personal, mental, and emotional growth was forgiveness. As we challenge the generational practices placed before us, the unlearning and relearning process must include forgiveness. In order to build a prosperous future, past transgressions need to be resolved
and released."
- Justin

Take time to reflect on the people and situations that have impacted you where you still have resentment. Try to identify how those actions influence your thoughts and behaviors today. Examples include but are not limited to distrust, lies you've been told, abusive relationships with family or romantic partners, etc.

Detail your process of recovery and how you are working to restore what you've lost in those moments of despair.

_____

_____

_____

_____

_____

_____

_____

_____

STEP 3
ACTION STEP

From the list of values below circle the ones that mean the most to you and guide your daily decisions. There are no rights or wrongs, just be honest!

1. Kindness
2. Integrity
3. Acceptance
4. Focus
5. Responsibility
6. Honesty
7. Commitment
8. Loyalty
9. Open-mindedness
10. Growth
11. Friendship
12. Faith
13. Knowledge
14. Leadership
15. Optimism
16. Spirituality
17. Sense of Community
18. Empathy
19. Respect
20. Perserverance
21. Gratitude
22. Curiosity
23. Blessing
24. Compromising
25. Adjusting
26. Truth
27. Trust
28. Respectful
29. Humility
30. Being true to yourself

Other values not listed that are important to you:

_____

_____

_____

Now that you have circled your values, try to reduce the number down to your top 5 of the ones you circled.

_____

_____

_____

_____

Which values are from your parents? Which ones were formed or validated through different stages of your life? Lastly, reflect on which of these aspects of love have you struggled with and how do you plan on growing in these areas?

_____

_____

_____

_____

_____

_____

_____

Now take time to reflect how much your values are shared by your partner and those in your community. How can you draw strengths and share weaknesses with each other as you push forward with new awareness?

"You are the fruit sent to the earth to develop as a tree, so the earth can eat from your fruit!"
- Myles Munroe

Reflect on the childhood version of you. What advice would you give to him or her as he/she prepares for the obstacles ahead? How would you strengthen him or her to overcome the barriers/challenges? Mentally? Emotionally? Spiritually? What change in perspective should they consider as they mature? What hope can you offer your childhood self?

_____

_____

_____

_____

Now that you have the armor and strength to build the pathway you desire, what will you do to continue the process of redefining normal? Consider your legacy and how your actions, thoughts, and motives impact others and start the process of becoming the change needed in your community and society overall.

Repeat after me: I am a trailblazer! I am an overcomer! God is FOR me! Greater is He that is within me than he that is in the world! I am healed and victorious in Jesus' name! Together, God and I are REDEFINING NORMAL!

"For we are God's masterpiece, created to do good works which God prepared in advance for us to do."
- Ephesians 2:10

REPEAT AFTER ME:
I AM A TRAILBLAZER!
I AM AN OVERCOMER!
I AM REDEFINING NORMAL!

ABOUT US

Justin Black created the Rising Over Societal Expectations (ROSE) Empowerment Group with a vision to close the information gap for today's generation of Black and Brown young adults after his experiences as a Black male in the foster care system. He has also developed policy recommendations while working with the National Black Child Development Institute resulting in a publication titled The State of the Black Child Report Card: Washington State.

Justin studied urban and community development as well as a political and economic philosophy in countries such as Rwanda, Uganda, Senegal, and South Korea. In his spare time, Justin loves watching sports and enjoys hot wings.

He aspires to challenge and expand the ideologies of how to build prosperous communities through interdependence and entrepreneurship.

Justin Black in

Alexis Lenderman-Black is a recent graduate of WMU with dual-degrees in Entrepreneurship and Global & International Studies with minors in nonprofit leadership and political science. Alexis published a bestselling book titled Redefining Normal: How Two Foster Kids Beat The Odds and Discovered Healing, Happiness, and Love with her husband, Justin Black. Now she operates three companies, Redefining Normal, ROSE (Rising Above Societal Expectations) Empowerment Group, and The Scholarship Expert. She hopes to encourage others to heal while breaking generational patterns to live a life worth living.

Alexis Lenderman-Black is a serial entrepreneur, bestselling author, and speaker. She currently co-operates five companies with her husband and published their best-selling book *Redefining Normal: How Two Foster Kids Beat The Odds and Discovered Healing, Happiness and Love*. She hopes to continue the conversations on breaking generational patterns and healing to help others live a life worth living.

in **Alexis Black**

STAY CONNECTED:

Facebook @redefiningnormalmovement
Instagram @re.definingnormal
re-definingnormal.com

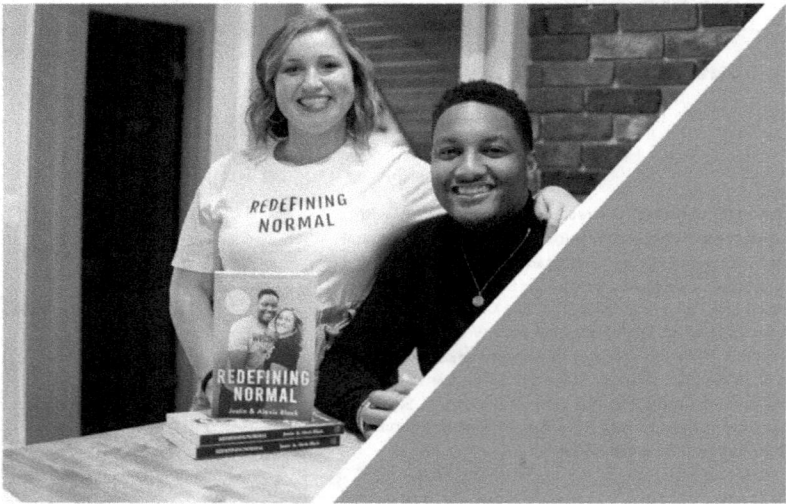

"Every kid is one caring adult away
from being a success story."
- Josh Shipp

LET'S REDEFINE NORMAL TOGETHER!

We would love to speak at your next event.
Book us here:

If you have any questions, feel free to email us at
speaking@re-definingnormal.com or call (248) 289-0844.